Memorial Hall Library
Andover, Mass. 01810

TRACK AND FIELD

TRACK

EDITED BY   DICK O'CONNOR

Jesse Owens

AND FIELD

NEW YORK   1976   ATHENEUM

Y
796.42
Owe

Library of Congress Cataloging in Publication Data

Owens, Jesse, 1913–
  Track and field.

  1. Track-athletics. I. Title. GV1060.5.093 796.4'2 76-11870
ISBN 0-689-10740-4

Composition by Connecticut Printers, Inc., Hartford, Connecticut
Printed and bound by Halliday Lithograph Corporation,
Hanover and Plympton, Massachusetts

Designed by Kathleen Carey
First Edition

Contents

TRACK AND FIELD

Warming Up

PREPARING FOR track and field competition is just as important as competing in the events themselves. You must be ready both mentally and physically for a race. If you're not, you can't win. It's as simple as that.

Begin by warming up properly. When I work with the San Francisco Giants baseball team in spring training, I tell them the body is like a rubber band. A rubber band will stretch to almost twice its length when it's warm and loose. But a rubber band that is cold will break if you try to stretch it too far.

In the same way the muscles in your legs and back and arms can stretch further when they are warm. When you need that extra bit of extension it's there.

3

Otherwise you might pull a muscle, like a rubber band snapping, and a pulled muscle can beat you as quickly as an opponent can.

There are four basic exercises that are good for warming up for all track and field events. They should be done at the start of each day's practice and will help you work on a specific event whether it's the 100-yard dash, running the mile, shot putting, or high jumping.

Try doing about 15 to 30 minutes a day of these exercises. You can devote 5 or 6 minutes to each exercise with a couple minutes of rest in between.

If you don't have that much time, you can do each one for 2 or 3 minutes. On warm days, it doesn't take as long to loosen up. The important thing is to stretch the muscles gently to avoid injury later. Remember these are just for warm-ups. To win you must practice the proper techniques of each event.

Here are the four exercises:

The *arm swing* gets the body in motion. It is essential in running or jumping to maintain your balance. In the 100-yard dash, for instance, a good arm swing will keep you moving forward at all times. This means that the runner who has mastered this technique can beat a faster runner who wastes motion by throwing his arms across his body.

To start the arm swing, drop the shoulders as low

4

The Arm Swing—Drop the shoulders as low as possible, swing the arms as though they were on pins driven through the shoulders. Keep the elbows at right angles and the body relaxed.

as possible. Then swing the arms as though they were on pins driven through the shoulders. Remember to keep the elbows at right angles and the body relaxed.

Increase the speed of the arm swing until you are going as fast as possible. Then swing them for a minute, rest for a minute, and do it again. About three one-minute arm swings will loosen up the arms and also teach you the proper motion used while running.

Remember, both the pole vaulter and high jumper can use this technique as well.

The second basic exercise is what I call the *knee-up*. It's really running in place, but the difference is

5

The Knee Up—Lift the knee high, staying on your toes.

in how high you lift the knees. High knee action is very important in proper running. In sprinting, keeping the knees up promotes a straighter body and keeps you from leaning back. It also keeps you moving forward in a straight line because the legs are kept in front of you.

The important thing when doing the knee-up is to stay on your toes. This helps you to run as lightly as possible rather than hitting the ground hard and flatfooted.

Also, by staying up on your toes, you have to lean a little forward, which helps keep the body moving forward.

6

Another important thing when doing the knee-up is to stay relaxed. You can't win a race if you're tense. Doing the knee-up helps relax the body.

The third basic exercise is the *knee pull*. It is just what it sounds like. Lift the right knee as high as possible in front of you and grasp it with both hands. Then pull it in as close to your chest as you can. Hold this position momentarily, then lower it. Repeat with the other leg.

Do not lean forward when doing this exercise. It is important to keep the back straight in order to run in an upright position. The knee pull helps develop speed and keeps you moving in a straight line. It prevents wasted motion that occurs when the legs are not kept in front while running. You can always tell a tired runner because his legs start to get out of control. The extra motion cuts down on speed and this loses the race.

The knee pull is also helpful in stretching the hip and thigh muscles. The thigh muscles are among the largest ones in the body and are easily strained if not properly prepared before a race. The knee pull is a simple exercise but a very effective one.

The final exercise is one that gets the whole body ready for competition. It is what I call *riding the bicycle* but is done while lying on the ground.

The exercise was made popular by Charley Pad-

Riding the Bicycle—Remember to lift your hips and legs as high as you can with just your neck and shoulders on the ground.

dock, who was known as the "world's fastest human" back in the 1930s.

First, lie down on your back. Then lift your hips and legs as high as you can with just your neck and shoulders on the ground. When you get into position, move your feet in a circular fashion as if riding a bicycle. This motion loosens up the joints in your legs and back and strengthens arm and back muscles. Because it strengthens the leg muscles as well, it is also a good exercise to quicken your leg action.

Once you complete these loosening-up exercises, you are ready to work on specific techniques.

I used to compete in several events and naturally had to practice all of them. But I found I could save some practice when the work I had done on one technique carried over and could be applied to another event. In both sprints and hurdles, for example, the start is basically the same. After practicing my starts for a while, I would jog a little to get my legs and body loose.

Then finally, I would get down to serious work on each event. For the sprints that meant running hard for a short distance.

It is very important to finish strong, so I always sprinted further than necessary. If I were preparing for the 100-yard dash, I would run at least 150 yards, or maybe even a little more. Then, when it was race time, I could run 100 yards hard and still be strong at the end.

But more about that later.

The main thing now is to have a practice schedule for each day and week of the season.

And then be sure to stick to it.

Conditioning

It doesn't make any difference how many warm-up exercises you do or how much talent you have if you're not in shape and physically fit. That's where discipline comes in.

When I was in seventh grade I ran a race against a ninth grader. I didn't run well, and after it was over, my coach sat me down and told me that I had given up in that race. He said I hadn't done the best I could, and I never forgot that. I made up my mind I would always try my best. Then, if I lost, I could congratulate the other runner, because he was truly better than I was and work hard to win the next time.

Another time I had pneumonia and missed several days of training. Afterward I tried to run in some races and lost. But losing this time didn't bother me because I knew I was not in good physical condition.

I realized then how important it is to be in good shape. You can't do your best if you're not. But every person is different. Some need more workout than others to get ready for a race. It's an individual thing, and only you can tell.

How much rest do you need? Again, you will have to determine the answer to that for yourself. Some people can get by on 6 hours of sleep and still function. Others need 8 and some people need as much as 10 hours. The important thing is to go to sleep when you are tired.

At this point I think something should be said about smoking, drinking, and sexual habits.

I know there is a great temptation to indulge when you are young. You see others doing it and think you can, too. That's when discipline becomes a factor again. You have to realize the harm smoking and drinking can have on your performance.

When you are in a race, stop to think about your opponent. Does he smoke or drink or dissipate himself in any way? If he does, you know you have a chance to beat him even though he may be a faster runner. And if you are the one smoking and drinking, you could lose to a runner who isn't as good as

11

you are. You are only cheating yourself when you don't follow good training habits.

Even if you win, think how much better you might have done if you didn't smoke or drink. Remember, you'll have many years after you're through competing to smoke and drink if you choose.

Your coach is a good person to listen to. My own coach taught me the three things that helped me be successful throughout my life: determination, dedication, and discipline.

A coach must be a good example to his athletes. He can't lie or they'll know immediately. In addition he must be a good psychologist.

To get the best from his athletes, he must treat them as individuals, adjusting his teaching methods according to their particular needs. And the athletes will profit by this, too.

The Dashes

THE MOST IMPORTANT thing in running the dashes, the 100, 200, and even the 440, is speed. It is something you either have or don't have.

Not every track man can be a sprinter. If you don't have natural speed, there probably is another event more suitable for you, such as a longer running race, the hurdles, or the long jump, to name a few.

I've always felt that the best way to win in this event is to run in as straight a line as possible. Every movement you make should be in front of you, toward the finish line. If you avoid excess motion, you can even beat a faster runner.

I like to think of the runner's arms as a pendulum

on a clock with the swinging motion in a straight line toward the finish.

Use your arms when you run. They swing naturally beside your body, but don't let them cut across your chest. This throws you off balance and creates a rocking motion that prevents you from driving ahead to the finish line.

Practice running with your foot pointing on a straight line toward the finish. It may sound funny, but it's not always easy to run a straight course. How often have you seen a sprinter lose a race because he didn't manage to do this?

That's where the four basic exercises I discussed will help. Each one will keep the body in a straight line—the arm swing, the knee-up, the knee pull, and the bicycling.

You have to remember that in track and field you are in an individual sport. It isn't like football where there are eleven people on a team, and if one person doesn't do his job, the others can make up for him.

When you are participating in sports like swimming, boxing, tennis, and track and field, you are out there on your own.

The coach can be your camera. He can tell you what you are doing wrong: if your head is steady, if your hands are going across your body, or if your knees are not coming up high enough.

14

That's where you have to listen and accept criticism. The coach can help you attain your goals.

Let's go through the basic steps in running the 100-yard dash.

First a word about starting blocks. This is one advantage runners of today have over runners of my time. We didn't have starting blocks. We dug little holes in the ground and put our feet into them to push off to get a quick start.

Begin by adjusting the starting blocks until they're comfortable for you. What may be right for one runner, doesn't necessarily work for another runner, so you'll just have to experiment on your own.

The start is probably the single most important thing in a race like the 100-yard dash. If you get off to a bad one, you don't have much chance of winning the race.

Once you get comfortable in the starting blocks, start thinking about how you are going to come out of them. This is something you can learn in practice.

Each day of the week before a meet, I used to get down in the blocks and practice about 5 or 6 starts. If you do this every day, it will become a natural motion.

Most runners usually start on their right feet. But if it feels more natural the other way around, take

This sprinter starts with his left foot. Notice the form: body straight, head up, and hands apart. You can see the initial drive he is generating.

your first step with your left foot, which is all right, too. Just do what is best for you.

The first 2 steps out of the block are very important. This is where you get your drive at the start.

Your hands should be far enough apart to keep them from bumping your body or legs as you come out of the blocks.

The body should stay straight as you start. Keep your head up and your back as straight as possible.

Once out of the blocks the only thing to think about is getting to the finish line as fast as you can.

All good runners look alike. They have to follow the same principles. We all ran the same way at my junior high school, because that was the way our coach taught us to run. You could watch 500 kids from Cleveland, Ohio, run, and you could pick out the ones who'd been taught by Coach Riley. They ran with their heads held firm and straight; they didn't look around.

All good sprinters today—the world-class sprinters—still run the same way.

The only difference is the finish. Back in my day, you had to get your chest across the finish line. Now, you can turn your shoulder into it and win. That's a good trick, turning your shoulder at the finish line.

You can lunge at the tape now. I was taught to run

through the tape and still think it's the best way.

To be a good 100-yard dash man, you have to run over that distance. You have to gear yourself to run 150 yards. You have to have a good start, accelerate in the middle of the race, and finish strong.

Once you get in full stride, your knees should be turning slightly inside to keep your legs on a straight line. The arms should swing the same way. I can't overemphasize the importance of moving in a straight line.

The 220-yard dash is basically the same as the 100. You are still running the race as fast as you can every step of the way. There isn't any pace to it. You just run as hard as you can.

The way to get ready for the 220 is to do overdistance running. Run some 660s and 880s with good speed. Then drop back down to your distance and run as hard as you can.

It is a question of building up a little more endurance than you need in the 100. You have to run just as hard in the 220 as you do in the 100. You just have to run a little farther.

Once you start in the 100, you usually pick up speed. This happens at the start when it takes a few strides to reach full speed. In running the 220, you're at full speed for more of the total distance.

You can see it in the times of the great sprinters.

They are actually running the 220 faster than the 100 because they're running their fastest for a longer distance. A runner who can run the 100-yard dash in 10 seconds should be able to run the 220 in less than 22 seconds. That's because when he reaches the 100-yard mark he is running at full speed. The extra 120 yards in the 220 is run at full speed. The same is true of any of the sprints, even the 440.

The 440 at one time was a pace race. Now it's an all out dash. The important thing to learn is how to stride a little because you have to run it on a turn. You need somewhat more durability also.

The 440 requires timing. It's a combination sprint and middle distance race. When you know how to time yourself, you become a better runner in an event like the 440. You can hold back a little and run with a smooth stride. In the 100 and 220 you don't have a chance to do that.

When you're running around a turn, you have to be careful not to get your legs tangled up.

You run a little looser than you do in the sprints. Your stride is longer and your arms may swing farther. But they still swing straight out in front.

The knees don't come up as high in the 440 as they do in the shorter sprints. The reason for this is that you stride more and take longer steps. It's really more of a glide than a power race like the 100 and 220.

There is a pace to the 440 that is not found in shorter sprints. Again only practice will determine what is the best speed for you to run this longer distance. You can also practice to make your pace faster. You will then be able to run the quarter mile faster, but at a pace you can maintain for the full distance.

But remember one basic thing.

Run in a straight line. Keep your toes pointed straight ahead toward the finish line and your arms swinging like a pendulum straight ahead of you.

When you get near the finish line, don't worry about what other runners are doing. Concentrate on finishing as fast as you can, and then look around at the others.

If your techniques are good ones, they should all be behind you.

Hurdles

LOW HURDLES are a speed event, whereas high hurdles require technique.

I feel that the start in the low hurdles is just as important as in the 100-yard dash. If you get off to a good one, you have a better chance to win.

Most of the same principles used in the sprints apply to the low hurdles. You have to use a high knee kick and swing your arms along at your sides in the direction of the finish line.

But hurdling is different when you come to the first jump.

The first thing to do is to understand the position you should be in while hurdling. The best way to do that is to sit down on the floor.

Place your legs out in front of you in the sitting position. Now decide which leg to put over the hurdle first. This will be your lead leg. It can be either your right or your left, whichever feels more natural.

Be sure the leg is extended straight in front of you, not pointed to the inside or the outside. Now tuck the other leg up beside you. That is the position your trailing leg will be in when you go over the hurdle.

With one leg in front and the other tucked up beside you, bend your back a little and extend your opposite hand to the toe of your lead leg. By that I mean that you reach out with your left hand if you are leading with your right leg. Or the opposite if you lead with your left leg.

Don't let the arm cross the body. It should be held as parallel as possible to the leg.

Now, bend over a few times and get the feeling of bringing your head down a little as your hand comes forward. This gives you the motion needed to go over the hurdle.

It is important to keep your eyes on the track ahead of you. Just because you bend your back and put your head down it is still important to watch where you are going. Now that you have an idea of where the legs should be as you go over the hurdles,

Your takeoff to the hurdle will be about 7 feet in front of it. Be sure your leg is extended straight in front of you. Now tuck the other leg up beside you. Extend the opposite hand to the toe of your lead leg.

go out on the track and try it.

Pay special attention to working on your starts so you know how many steps it takes to get to the first hurdle. Normally, it's about 7, but for smaller people, it might be 8.

Your takeoff to the hurdle will be about 7 feet in front of it. The exact distance may be determined when you start running the hurdles at full speed.

You can start by walking through it and counting the number of steps it takes and then see how many are needed to come out of the starting blocks.

Once out of the blocks run at full speed toward the hurdles. When you get to your seventh or eighth step it will be time to jump.

Get your lead leg out in front of you. Make sure you lift it high enough to clear the hurdle. If you don't clear, it doesn't make any difference how fast you are or how much technique you have. You can't win by hitting hurdles.

As you come up to the first hurdle, keep your eye on the top of it so you know how high to go. Then, as soon as you know you're over the hurdle, concentrate on getting your trailing leg on the ground as fast as possible and look for the next hurdle.

The knee of the trailing leg has to be pointed in the direction of the finish line. This helps get your foot back on the ground more quickly.

Don't float over the hurdle. It's much faster to move on the ground than it is to float through the air. Also, if you're slow getting back on the ground, you could lose a fraction of a second, which could lose the race.

Your arms will help you get over the hurdle, too. Thrusting the left arm out, if you lead with your right leg, it will pull you up and over. The arm should be close to the body and not waving about in the air. That just slows you down.

The hurdles are 10 yards apart, and all you have room for are 3 steps before you take the next hurdle. It's hurdle, one-two-three, and hurdle again. The important thing here is to develop the same technique for going over each hurdle.

First, be ready to jump as soon as you take that third step. Then clear the first hurdle with your right foot as the lead leg, and snap your left foot back on the ground quickly.

Your first step after the hurdle is a right, then a left, and another right before you take off.

On that fourth stride you are on your way over the next hurdle.

Remember: the important thing is to clear the hurdle. Don't hurry and hit one. You can't win the race if you fall.

If everything is going all right, you should pick up

speed as you go along and get into the groove.

I think you'll find that if you concentrate on getting over the first hurdle in good form, the rest will follow naturally.

The low hurdles is almost a dash with slight jumps along the way. You don't need much lift to clear them, nor do you have to bend over a great deal.

The high hurdles take more concentration. It isn't always the fastest runner who wins in the high hurdles; it's the one with the best form.

You can save time on each high hurdle by getting the trailing leg back on the ground as soon as possible to take off for the next hurdle.

Once you clear the last hurdle—either in the highs or the lows—concentrate on the finish line. Don't look around to see where the other contestants are. That will only slow you down. If you've run the race with the proper form, you'll win. Then when you get to the finish line, run the same way as you would in the 100-yard dash. Don't let up.

Run through the tape. You might gain a fraction of a second by turning your shoulder into the tape. And fractions of seconds are what determine the winners.

How do you practice for the hurdles? I found the best way to do it was to work on my starts every day.

Each day, I would practice a start and then go over the first 2 hurdles several times. Run it hard . . . all out.

Get those first 2 driving strides from the starting blocks to get you over the first hurdle. Then one-two-three again and stop short of the third hurdle. All you really need for practice is the technique of getting over that first hurdle and the proper stride for the second one.

The strides are a little more important in the high hurdles than lows, so you might want to go over 3 hurdles.

At least once during practice each day, run a complete flight of hurdles at full speed. Then do some overdistance running.

If you're competing in the 220-yard low hurdles, run some 440s. Jog even further than that. But run a hard quarter mile at least once each day during practice.

If you're running the 100-yard high hurdles, run some 220-yard dashes and then jog some quarter miles.

Another thing: have a teammate or the coach watch you go over the hurdles to find out by how much you are clearing them.

You should be just skimming over, almost touching the top. The closer you come to the hurdle without hitting it, the more time you save. As I said before, the biggest loss of time in this event comes when you float over rather than thrust that lead leg over and snap the trailing leg down as fast as you can.

At this point I would like to say something about breathing while running the hurdles. Take a deep breath just before you start the race and another just before you finish. You might take the second deep breath as you clear the final hurdle. Then you'll have some extra strength for the final sprint to the finish line. That's where many hurdles races are won.

Balance is also key in running the hurdles. If you run off balance you might hit one and fall.

Use your arms to help you with this. Keep them thrusting out in front of you, not too far from the body but always in a pendulum motion toward the finish line.

The great low hurdlers also do quite well in the sprints. They need speed.

The high hurdlers are more graceful. The most graceful high hurdler I ever saw was Lee Calhoun, who won Olympic gold medals in Melbourne in 1956 and Rome in 1960. He seemed to glide over them in perfect form. But he also had the speed and grace of a great hurdler.

And of course, speed is important. I remember in

1948 when Harrison Dillard, the greatest high hurdler in the world, failed to make the United States Olympic team when he hit a hurdle. But he was fast enough to make the team in the 100-yard dash. He surprised everyone by winning the gold medal in the 100 at the Olympics in London that year.

So it takes both style and speed to be a great hurdler. It takes more speed in the lows and more style in the highs. But regardless of which event you are competing in, you need some of both.

Another hurdle event, the intermediates, is a little different from the highs and lows. It still requires speed and technique, but endurance is also a factor here. You need the speed of a sprinter, the style of a high hurdler, and the endurance of a quarter miler. The best intermediate hurdler to my mind was Glenn Davis, who won gold medals in two different Olympics. He had all three of these requirements: speed, style, and endurance.

It is not a race where you can pace yourself. Like the 440-yard dash, you have to run the whole race all out, as fast as you can.

The principles for the intermediate hurdles are the same as for the other hurdle events: get a good start and know your strides.

After that it's a matter of running as fast as you can and making sure you don't hit anything. Once again, thrust the lead leg over the hurdle and snap your trailing leg back down as fast as you can.

Also remember to synchronize your arms and legs to keep your balance.

The intermediates is one of the most difficult events in track and field. It's for the athlete who isn't quite fast enough for the sprints, not quite graceful enough for the high hurdles, and a little too slow for the 440-yard dash.

It takes determination. And if you have that, plus dedication and discipline, you can win in track and field.

The Distance Races

DETERMINATION IS THE KEY to being a good distance runner. The mile runner needs more self-command than a sprinter, broad jumper, or weight lifter.

Distance runners usually don't have great speed but have considerable endurance instead. A good mile runner learns to pace his running speed, unlike a sprinter who just runs as fast as he can from the start.

The only way to find your own pace is to run. Start out by running the full distance, whether it be the mile, two miles, or even longer races. Your original running time for the mile might be 6 minutes. Once you can run at that pace, work on your

33

speed. Gradually you'll be able to lower your time.

In running the mile, the start is just as important as in the sprints. The way you begin a race is, I believe, the way you'll finish it. If you use good running techniques from the outset, they should stay with you all the way.

Some great milers are fast starters. They build up a big lead and then use whatever they have left to finish the race. Other milers are strong finishers. They have a last-lap "kick" to overtake other runners.

But the best way to run a race is strong and steady from beginning to end. If you stay in good position, there won't be any need to "kick" at the end. Also, you won't have to worry about burning out before the finish line.

Paavo Nurmi, the Finnish runner, was a great pacer. He could tell you, almost to the exact second, how fast he was running at any point in the race.

In a mile race, there will be someone to tell you the time as you complete each lap. This will help you judge your pace.

If you plan to run a mile in 4 minutes, 10 seconds, the time for the first lap should be about 62 seconds. The second and third laps might be a little slower, depending on your pace. Your last lap should be a little faster, perhaps less than a minute. Give it all

34

the energy you have left.

But, once again, be sure you have enough left to finish. Many a mile race has been lost because a runner faded in the last few yards after setting too fast a pace.

Although some of the principles are the same, distance running differs from sprinting in several ways. In running the mile, it is important to conserve energy. The arms don't swing as high as they do in shorter races. The high knee lift isn't feasible in distance running because of the endurance required just to finish. But a smooth stride is essential. The legs just barely get off the ground.

To conserve energy, run on the balls of your feet rather than the toes as you would in the sprints. Don't run on your heels.

As in sprinting, always keep the body moving straight toward the finish line.

In a distance race, breathing is critical. You must keep as much oxygen as possible in the body. Oxygen provides energy and keeps the blood circulating.

Run loose. Tension cuts off circulation and puts a strain on your body. Also avoid clenching your fists while you run. This restricts the blood from going back to the heart. The best distance runners are the ones who run relaxed.

Once you get off to a good start, settle into the

35

pace that is best for you. Don't worry about the other runners. There might be a "rabbit" who will try to get you to run faster than you really should.

Run as close to the inside of the track as possible. If you're out in the middle you'll have a greater distance to cover. In a mile race, all competitors are entitled to the inside lane. It isn't like the sprints where each runner must stay in his own lane.

Avoid being boxed in behind other runners. Leaving the rail to overtake other runners squanders your energy.

When you get into that final sprint for the finish line, don't worry about your opponents. Don't try to speed up just because they do. Stick to your own pace.

The best training for distance running is to run as much as you can.

The 100-yard dash man should run 200 yards to develop a strong finish. The 220-yard man should run a quarter mile to develop his strength. And the miler might run 4 miles a day, though occasionally he should run shorter distances to develop speed.

The two-mile run is basically the same as the mile, except that it calls for a shorter stride because of the added distance.

It also calls for a smoother pace. Almost every lap is run at the same speed, which means it isn't too often you will see two milers with a finishing kick.

Remember, decide what pace is best for you and then stick to it.

Relays

THE RELAY RACES are the only team events in track and field. I always enjoyed running the relays because it was fun to feel you were helping your teammates.

Sometimes one member of the team might not be fast enough to win an event by himself. But he can be a valuable contributor to a relay team all the same and share in the fun of winning.

The sprint relay is the 440-yard race, once around the track. The team for this is made of of 100- and 220-yard dash men, with each man running a 110-yard lap. The key to the 440 relay is speed and good baton passing.

The 880-yard relay team is also made up of sprinters, and again, a quick baton pass is essential for success.

A team for the mile relay is made up of quarter milers and half milers. There are times when a strong 220-yard man might also be on the team. Each man runs 440 yards.

The longer relays are for the distance men. In the four-mile race, each runner covers a mile, and there isn't as much emphasis on baton passing in this event. If you lose a second wtih an imperfect pass, the next runner has more than 4 minutes to make it up.

But by no means underestimate the importance of a good baton pass. It is often the crucial element in relay racing and can make the difference between winning and losing. In the 440-yard relay, a team of four sprinters who can run around 9.8 or 9.9 for the 100 can lose to four runners who are 10.0-flat runners if they exchange the baton better.

You can lose half a second with a slow pass. If the next runner has to wait to get the baton, he will not be running at top speed when he starts. If the first runner slows down before he hands the baton to the second runner, there will also be a time loss.

The worst thing is to drop the baton. To avoid such a calamity, take a fraction of a second longer to

Baton Passes—Various techniques but each employing the same basic principles as those set forth in the text.

insure that the next runner has received the baton safely.

Relay runners have a clearly marked 20-yard passing lane in which to make the exchange. If you pass it beyond that area, your team will be disqualified.

Practice baton exchanges with an eye on the markers. Too often, even in the Olympics, teams are disqualified because they pass out of the legal zone.

I think the exchange should be made at the first opportunity. I realize there are several methods to do this, but, for the beginner, I think the simplest way is the best.

While waiting for the baton, look back to see where your teammate is. Signal him by waving your hand so he is aware of your position. Then, when he gets to the point you've already selected, take 2 quick steps and reach back for the baton.

Your hand should be opened flat behind you when taking the baton. The runner who is passing should concentrate on putting it right across the center of the next runner's hand. The second runner should firmly grasp the baton as soon as he feels it.

If your timing is right, the first runner should be running at top speed when he hands the baton to the next runner.

There should be no delay. But again this is where practice can make all the difference.

On the 2 steps before receiving the baton, make sure you're running in a straight line. Sometimes relay races are lost because runners bump into each other. If it's one of your own teammates, you'll lose time, but if it's a runner from another team, you could be disqualified.

Some teams have their runners start from a sprinter's position as they wait for the baton. The second runner looks back through his legs and takes off when the runner behind him gets to a certain set point. This method might gain an extra fraction of a second if the baton exchange is perfect. But there's also the chance of dropping it.

The runner passing the baton should get a good grip on the bottom half until the next runner grasps the top half firmly. The second runner should take the baton with his right hand and switch it to his left as soon as possible, usually after 1 stride.

The best and safest way to do this is to bring the baton up in the right hand in front of the chest. Then with the left hand get a grip on the bottom half of the baton. Once you've accomplished this, the only thing to do is concentrate on running.

Another method of exchanging the baton is for the second runner to start further back in the passing zone. When the first runner gets within 5 yards of the zone, the second runner starts running.

After about 10 yards, both runners should be running at the same speed. The receiving runner places his right hand next to his hip with the palm up. This makes a pocket for the first runner to place the baton in.

Once the second runner feels the baton securely in his hand, he takes off, switching the baton to his left hand as soon as possible.

If the first runner says "Go" when he feels ready to hand over the baton, the second runner will be able to anticipate the transfer more accurately.

Whichever method you use to exchange the baton, there is no reason to look back at the incoming runner once you've started running.

The make-up of a relay team can mean the difference between winning and losing. The coach must decide what each member does best.

The standard make-up of a team has the second fastest runner as lead-off man. The third fastest goes second, and the slowest runner goes third.

The anchor man, or last runner, should be the fastest so that he can make up any time the third runner might lose.

The United States usually does well in relay races at the Olympics. In the 1936 Olympics in Berlin, for example, the United States had a very good 400-meter relay team made up of Floyd Draper, Frank Wycoff, Ralph Metcalfe, and myself.

Our coach decided that I would be the lead-off man because he wanted us to get a good start, also because the first runner doesn't have too much of a curve to run.

I handed the baton to Metcalfe and he ran the back stretch where he handed the baton to Draper, who was our best runner on curves.

Then Wycoff finished up. He was a great front runner and no one could catch him when he had the lead. He just pulled away from the other runners on the final leg and we won the gold medal.

Our time was 40 seconds flat, which tied the existing Olympic record set by the U.S. team in Los Angeles in 1932. That record was not broken until 1956, when the American team of Ira Murchison, Leamon King, Thane Baker, and Bobby Morrow did 39.5 in Melbourne, Australia.

Weight Events

As I said before, there is something for everyone in track and field. The weight events—the shot put and the discus—are for stronger individuals. But let me point out that even weight men need speed.

The shot put changed dramatically with Parry O'Brien back in the 1950s. Previously, shot putters started by facing the area where they were going to throw.

O'Brien, who won gold medals in the 1952 Olympics in Helsinki, Finland, and again in the 1956 games in Melbourne, Australia, changed all that. He found that by turning his back before throwing, he gained the power of a body turn and could get more of his weight behind the throw. He also realized that the speed with which he got across the shot-put ring gave him a longer throw.

That's why speed is important in the weight events just as in every other track and field event.

Before you even put the shot, remember to save as much energy as possible for each put. There are some easy tricks shot putters use to do this. For instance, if you are a right-handed shot putter, carry the shot in your left hand until ready to throw. This will keep your right arm from getting tired. Once you get in the ring take your position for the put, then change the shot from your left hand to your right.

The shot should not rest in the palm of your hand. It should be out on the tips of the fingers in order to get more thrust.

The middle three fingers of the hand should be on the back side of the shot. The thumb and little finger should support the shot from the front side.

When the shot is thrown, the thrust comes from the three middle fingers with the outer fingers acting as directional guides.

Now you're ready to go into the shot-put ring. It is best to walk through the put, step by step, before actually throwing.

Take a position in the back of the ring with your right foot against the back line. Move your left foot

47

toward the front. The distance between your feet should be approximately 2 feet. The important thing is to have a comfortable stance.

Rest the shot put against your shoulder and neck. Now you are ready for the hop across the ring that will launch the shot.

As in the high jump, you'll get better results by putting a little spring in the body. In the shot put, the more body weight you get behind the put, the further you'll be able to throw.

When you're ready, get into a crouch position with most of your weight on the right leg. This will allow you to move quickly across the right with your left, or lead, leg.

Keep your body in line as much as you can to generate forward power. The shoulders should be square over your hips to get the most weight under and behind the throw.

The move across the ring is more of a slide than a hop. The left foot should slide across the ring and the right leg should provide the push-off.

Some competitors find it better to swing the left leg back before sliding across the ring. Others find that lifting the left leg and then going forward is more natural.

Once again, use whichever method feels best for you. Your coach can help decide which of the two

48

Take a position in the back of the ring with your right foot against the back line. Rest the shot against your shoulder and neck.

(BELOW) When you're ready, get into a crouch position with most of your weight on the right leg.

The move across the ring is more of a slide than a hop.

As you cross the ring the shot still rests against your neck and shoulder.

The shot is thrown with a flip of the fingertips as the arm is thrust out full length. Concentrate on staying in the ring.

styles is better. He can also watch your footwork and make any necessary adjustments.

Once you work out the footwork, you are ready to put the shot.

As you cross the ring, the shot put still rests against your neck and shoulder. It should be put just as both your feet touch ground after sliding across the ring.

First, take an upright position by straightening the legs as you come out of the crouch. Turn slightly to the left as you straighten up.

The left arm goes back in a motion which pulls the right side of the body toward the target. The right arm goes up and out with the elbow directly behind the shot.

Keeping the weight behind the shot prevents arm strain and gives maximum distance. The shot is thrown with a flip off the fingertips as the arm is thrust out full length. The shot rolls off into a high arc to obtain the greatest distance.

If the shot put is made correctly, you should feel a surge of power through the body from the legs to the ends of the fingers.

As soon as the shot has left your hand, concentrate on staying in the ring. Many great shot puts have been disqualified because of a misplaced foot.

The best way to make sure you stay in the ring is

to shift your weight from the right to the left foot and turn away from the direction the shot has been thrown. If you turn the big right toe to the left at the front of the ring, it will help your entire body move left to avoid fouling.

A common mistake shot putters make is to watch the throw after it has been made. This tends to make you lean forward, and perhaps step out of the ring.

Carelessness can also cause a foul. Make sure, after the put is made, to leave the ring at the back. It's a technicality, but going out the front, even after the put has been completed, may result in a foul.

The discus throw is similar to the shot put in that both require strength and speed, but to throw the discus a little more technique is needed as well. It also helps to have big hands, though, of course, it's not a prerequisite.

In grasping the discus make sure to have the center as close as possible to the center of your hand. If your hands are large, it's easy. If they're small, a slight adjustment is needed.

The thumb should be on the side of the discus to provide balance and direction.

A good way to start throwing is from a 90-degree angle to the direction you will be throwing.

A few preliminary swings of the arm will relax the body and get you ready for the actual throw. The

Grasp the discus with the center of your hand as close as possible to the center of the discus. The thumb should be on the side for balance and direction. Start at a 90° angle to the direction in which you will be throwing. After a couple of swings, pivot, making sure your feet are firm on the ground. Keep the body low in a comfortable crouch. Keep the discus above the waist at all times. The entire throwing motion should be in one piece, with no stopping. A complete follow-through is essential.

motion should be back and forth with the discus balanced in your hand.

After a couple of swings, when you feel ready to throw, pivot, making sure your feet are firm on the ground. This is unlike the shot put where you slide across the ring.

In the pivot the body stays in a low, but comfortable, crouch.

The right arm, if that is the one you are throwing with, remains behind the right side until the pivot is completed and the throw is ready to be made. Be sure not to dip the discus too low. It should never go below the waistline.

The entire throwing motion should be in one piece with no stopping. The power surge should come right through the body from the legs and into the hand, as the discus is whipped toward the target area.

The arm should be fully outstretched at its highest point before letting go of the discus.

This is where your coach can help. He can watch the pivot and the position of the legs and arms as you swing through the motion.

Just like golf, once the discus leaves your hand, take care to follow through completely. If you stop as soon as the throw is made, you won't get any momentum behind the discus. If your body continues to turn after the throw, you'll get a longer throw.

As in the shot put, your feet must stay within the circular boundaries.

Another important point: make sure the discus is moving slightly upward as it leaves your hand. You can't make a good throw if the discus goes into the ground.

Wind is another big factor in throwing the discus. You will have to make allowances for it. Once again, think of golf. When the wind is behind you, hit the ball high. When it's against you, keep the ball low to avoid "hanging" in the air.

If the wind is blowing from behind you, it can help make the discus go farther. Your throw must be slightly higher than normal to take advantage of this. If the wind is blowing toward you, a lower throw will help get maximum distance. The discus will cut through the wind.

I must emphasize that speed is important in events like the shot put and discus throw. In the shot put, arm speed and quick leg movement will help get the best effort. In the discus throw, arm speed in the pivot will result in a longer throw.

Both the shot-put and the discus are specialized events. Your coach can help you make the adjustments necessary to achieve top performance.

Javelin Throw

I HAVE ALWAYS ADMIRED javelin throwers because their event is like no other in track and field.

It is the only event that combines both running and throwing. It is different from the discus and shot put, the other throwing events, because they are done from basically a stationary position.

The javelin takes some foot speed, a strong arm, and perfect coordination. It looks easy until you try it. But the combination of running with a spear in your hand, then stopping and throwing it while maintaining balance is something that only the most coordinated athletes can do.

The javelin is one of the oldest of all track events. It goes back to the ancient days when man hunted with a spear. In those days, a poor spear thrower didn't get anything to eat. Now, the good spear thrower gets a gold medal in a track meet.

Like so many track events, the easiest way to understand the principle is to walk through it.

Grasp the javelin comfortably in the palm of your hand. It's difficult to hold one incorrectly because of the cord grip on it.

Now get the feel of running with the javelin. The best way to hold it is at your side, then lift it above your shoulder.

Next try running a few steps with the javelin at head level. In order to keep it in rhythm with your steps, you'll need to practice.

Notice that the natural swing of the javelin as you run is back and forth. After a little practice, you should be able to coordinate your steps with this motion.

As you run with the javelin take care not to let it dip down too much in the front or rear.

How far should you run before releasing the javelin? That depends on several things. If you are big and strong, a long run probably isn't necessary. Your arm will be strong enough to get a good throw without a long run. But if you are smaller, a long run can increase the momentum of the throw. About 75 feet is an average run before throwing.

Some javelin throwers find using check marks helpful. That way they can time their run somewhat better. But I think it depends on individual preference.

The single most important part of throwing the javelin is the crossover step. The crossover step puts you in the correct position to get off the left foot as you release the javelin. It is not a natural motion, and takes a great deal of practice to perfect.

The first part of the crossover comes when your right foot is 25 to 30 feet from the foul line. As your right foot comes down, lean the body back just a little to put the javelin into position for throwing. Then step with your left foot slightly to the right.

The next step is the crossover with your right foot going across in front of your left and keeping the toes pointed back to the left.

It is a difficult step . . . one of the toughest in any track and field event.

At this point your arm should be as far back as you can get it with the javelin ready to come forward in the thrust that will end in throwing and releasing.

The left arm will extend out in front, high enough to maintain your balance, which may be offset by the body leaning backward and the drag of the javelin behind.

At the same time extend the right arm fully, pre-

61

A left-handed javelin throw employs the same technique described in the text for right-handed throwers. Just substitute left foot for right and vice-versa.

paring to throw. Also make sure the right hand is facing up and in position for the throw.

Then take a long step with your left foot. Your feet will still be fairly wide apart to allow your hips to pivot as you make the throw.

As your right foot hits the ground on the next step, your right knee locks in a straight position to give you the proper push-off.

With your right foot planted, the right arm starts forward in a motion similar to a tennis player serving the ball. The hand should be high over the shoulder to get the fullest extension and follow through.

If your feet are properly planted, you can feel your strength running through the body and into the arm for the throw.

The only thing left now is to guide the javelin in the proper direction with the fingers. Much like a baseball pitcher, the power comes from the arm but the control is from the fingertips.

If the javelin is released at the correct moment, it will soar through the air, level off in midflight, and start downward into the ground.

The only way to get the feeling of the proper javelin throw is by repetition.

Keep practicing the crossover step and releasing the javelin.

As I have said, it is a difficult movement. The only way to make it feel more natural is by constant practice.

Throwing the javelin for distance is similar to hitting a golf ball. If the wind is blowing in your face, the throw should be a little lower than normal. If you have the wind behind you, take advantage of it by throwing the javelin with more loft than usual.

One of the prettiest sights in track and field is watching the spear soar through the air and stick in the ground.

Remember not to foul. The best way to do that is to allow plenty of room behind the foul line. The right foot should be on the ground with the left foot trailing, then swinging up and back after the javelin is released. This will help you keep your balance after the throw so there is less chance of fouling.

There was a very good javelin thrower a few years ago named Al Cantello. He would leap forward and land on his chest and stomach after throwing the javelin. It was a unique style that he found best suited him. I feel, however, the basic method of throwing and staying on your feet is probably best for most beginners.

Pole Vault

I CONSIDER THE pole vault to be the toughest event in all of track and field.

It takes more skill to do well than any other. The great pole vaulter has to have the speed of a sprinter, the strength of a weight lifter, and the agility of a gymnast. A little knowledge of physics also helps. In addition, the pole vault probably requires more practice than other events.

Pole vaulting is the only track and field event in which you are allowed to use something to help you achieve your goal.

The pole vault has changed over the years. When I was competing, it took more strength than it does now. You used either a bamboo or steel pole and

66

you had to vault over the bar. Now, with the fiberglass pole, it is more of an acrobatic event. Because a fiberglass pole bends, timing is very important. You have to push away from the pole and over the bar at just the right moment. That's where physics comes in. You have to know exactly when to let the pole get you over the bar.

The start of the pole vault is the same as a sprint. You must run as fast as possible to get maximum takeoff with the pole.

Pole vaulters need strong arms and shoulders so they can carry the pole and swing away from it.

Good balance is also essential to a pole vaulter. You need balance to run with the pole and balance to go up and over the bar.

It's important to have a pole you can handle. They come in different sizes and you must find the one that suits you best. Ask your coach for help.

Where do you grip the pole? Stand the pole next to the crossbar at the height you are attempting to clear. Place your right hand on the pole at approximately the point where it touches the crossbar. Your thumb will be over the top and on the outside, with the other fingers underneath the pole, facing the pit.

Place the left hand about 2 feet below the right one on the pole. It doesn't have to be exact; the correct grip is the one most comfortable for you.

67

The pole is gripped with your hand about 2 feet apart. When the pole hits the takeoff, you should be coming down on your left foot.

Once the pole is planted, swing the body forward, with the right leg starting to go up.

Bend your knees a little to help swing your body upward. The body turns somewhat as you swing and this helps get your legs in position to go over the bar first.

First push with the left arm, then with the right. The left hand comes off the pole first. Then let go with your right. Get your hands and arms over the crossbar as soon as possible.

The left-hand fingers are on top of the pole with the thumb underneath.

Once you determine the grip points, tape them to get a better hold.

The basic grip is used regardless of the height you are trying to jump. The only difference is that the grip will be higher on the pole as you attempt to clear the raised crossbar.

The run up for the pole vault is usually about 100 feet. It can be shorter or longer depending on the individual.

This is one event in which I think check marks are important. There should be one at the point where you start, and another one about 12 feet, or 2 strides, from your starting point. A third check mark should be about 60 feet from the takeoff point. You should come to each of the last two check marks on your left foot, which will be your takeoff foot.

In the run up, the pole is kept as parallel to the ground as possible. It may be slightly down in front to help get it into the vaulting box.

Start running down the runway at top speed as soon as possible. Maintain this speed until you are 2 or 3 strides from the vaulting box.

At this point, your entire concentration should be on getting the pole in the box properly.

When you feel the pole hit the takeoff box, you

74

should be coming down on your left foot and ready to take off.

It is important to get these things down perfectly. You can't vault if the pole isn't in the box as your takeoff foot hits the ground.

Once the pole is planted, every movement is in swinging up onto the pole and over the bar. You swing the body forward as the right leg starts to go up. Bend your knees a little to help swing your body upward.

Your body turns somewhat as you swing and this helps get your legs in position to go over the bar first. Now wait for the exact moment to push away from the pole and go over.

The arms should be bent a little at the elbow to give you strength to push off. First push with the left arm, then with the right. The left hand also comes off the pole first. Then let go with your right hand. Get your hands and arms over the crossbar as soon as possible.

Now that you are up there, how do you get down? As quickly and safely as possible. This is where it helps to be a gymnast. You have to land lightly to prevent injury. The knees should be bent slightly on landing to absorb the impact shock. Remember, if you clear the bar at 15 or 16 feet, that's a long way to come down.

75

Pole vaulting is not easy. As I said before, it is probably the most difficult of all events in track and field. But it is also one of the most rewarding. What a great feeling to land safely in the pit and look back up at that crossbar still in place.

Same sequence from behind the vaulter.

The High Jump

WITH THE POSSIBLE exception of the pole vault, no event has changed more in the last few years than the high jump.

When I first started high jumping, and that was long ago, we used the *Eastern roll*. This involved a scissor movement in which you jumped as high as you could and then scissored, or spread, your legs over the bar. There was a limit to how high you could jump because you had to lift your body after you got one leg over the bar.

Then along came the *Western roll*. Here the jumper dives over the bar and pulls his legs behind him. Many inches were added to the world record with this innovation.

The basic ingredient in the high jump is the run up to the bar. If you complete the approach properly, you have a chance of clearing the bar. But if it's done incorrectly, there's no way you'll clear it.

How long should the run up be? It can vary for different jumpers. The average number of steps is 9 or 10.

When you start your run the body should be at a 45-degree angle to the bar. This gives you the maximum lift for takeoff.

It is best to walk through the event first. Get an idea of how many steps you need to reach the take-off spot. To do this, stand next to the high-jump bar, leaning your body at a 45-degree angle, and reach out an arm's length to the bar. This distance is just about right.

If you're any closer, you may hit the bar on the way up and knock it off. If your takeoff is too far away, you'll come down either in front of it or on top of it.

However, you may find it better to stand a few inches closer or farther away. You'll have to figure out what's best for you.

The last 3 steps in the high jump are the most important. These give you the lift needed to clear the bar.

If you are right-handed, take your last step before

83

When you start your run the body should be at a 45° angle to the bar. If you are right-handed, take your last step before jumping with your left foot.

Swing your right leg as high as you can toward the bar. This will pull the body up.

As you rise, tuck the left leg in as close to the body as you can. While clearing the bar, keep your body almost parallel to it, with the legs close together. Once you are over, lower your head as soon as possible.

When you feel yourself clearing the bar turn your body to face the ground.
Make sure you land on your hands and left leg. Keep your palms toward the
ground. When the right leg comes along, roll over onto the foam rubber pit.

jumping with your left foot. Then swing your right leg as high as you can toward the bar. This will pull the body up.

The last stride before takeoff should be slightly longer than the ones before it. This will slow you down just a little and help you get up in the air.

Balance is very important in the high jump. You should have your body directly above your takeoff foot when you start to jump.

If you lean too far forward, there is a good chance of hitting the bar on the way up. If you lean backward, you probably will hit the bar as you go over it.

Your leg swing can be done two ways. Some very good jumpers keep the leg straight. Others believe in bending it slightly. Once again, decide for yourself which is best.

Your arms are important in providing the lift you need to clear the bar. If you take off from your left foot and swing your right leg up, your left arm should also swing up at the same time. This will force you to pull the body up and over the bar.

As you rise, tuck the left leg in as close to the body as you can. Many great jumps have been ruined because the bar was knocked off by that trailing leg.

While clearing the bar, keep your body almost parallel to it with the legs close together.

89

Once you're over, lower your head as soon as possible. Also lower your left arm after it clears the bar. This action of the head and left arm will give the rest of your body a little more lift.

When you feel yourself clearing the bar, turn your body to face the ground. This is the Western roll.

Now think about landing, which is just as important as taking-off.

Bend your arms somewhat and keep your palms toward the ground. Make sure you land on your hands and left leg.

Then, when the right leg comes along, roll over onto the foam rubber of the pit.

If everything goes well, you should be able to look up and find the crossbar still up where it belongs.

Remember one thing: A good jump can be ruined because of carelessness. Don't relax your arms or legs as you go over the bar. This can cause you to knock off the crossbar with your hand or your foot.

If I were teaching someone to high jump, I would start with the bar at about 2 feet. I would have him run up to the bar with the proper stride and take a nice easy roll over it.

Once you have the idea how to get over the bar correctly, simply work on getting more spring and lift as the bar is moved higher.

The big change in the high jump came in the early 1970s, when a jumper from Oregon State University named Dick Fosbury popularized a new style, now known as the *Fosbury Flop*.

Fosbury was a 6-foot-7-inch high jumper using his own ''backward'' style of jumping. His coach at Oregon State felt he could never improve this way and tried to convert him to the normal straddle method of jumping. Instead of getting better, Fosbury found himself growing worse. When he had trouble clearing 6 feet, Fosbury and his coach decided to go back to the ''flop'' style of jumping again.

The Fosbury Flop is basically opposite to any other style of high jumping. Instead of running at the bar from a 45-degree angle, the approach is at an arc from the side. The jumper lines up about 45 feet from the bar and 19 feet to the left of the left upright that supports the crossbar.

The jumper then runs in an arc toward the bar. The first few steps are run on a line toward the left rear of the landing pit.

Then, as the jumper nears the bar, he moves into an arc that brings him parallel to the bar. The last 3 steps are run in this parallel fashion, and with the final 2, the hips are lowered to prepare for the upward thrust of the body.

If the approach is from the left, then take off with the left foot. Once it hits, the right leg is pulled upward as hard as possible. At the same time, thrust the left arm to provide lift.

The rotation of the body comes from moving the left leg away from the bar at takeoff. This keeps the point of balance beneath the body and forces an upward movement.

The left knee lifts and crosses over the bar, pulling the body along with it. By cutting down on the body's rotation, there is no loss of lift by rolling over the bar as in other methods of high jumping.

Once the jumper gets up to the bar, the head is lowered against the chest and the shoulders are shrugged to pull them over the bar.

Then, if everything has been done right, you should soar over the bar without losing any of the approach momentum.

The physics involved in this technique is quite simple. All of the upward thrust is maintained because there is a minimum of body twist in going over the bar.

In the flop, the body remains over the legs to provide upward thrust through the head and shoulders.

The "flop" style isn't as smooth as some other

methods of high jumping. But it has proved most effective. All of the world-class jumpers use it.

World-record holder Dwight Stones, who has cleared 7 feet, 6½ inches, uses this "flop" style of high jumping. "You are able to generate more speed in that style," Stones said. "When I jump, I continue in the line I have created on the run. My body just follows the line. It's physics. I always think 'up'—the arms go up, the knees go up, the foot goes up, so the body has to go up. Everything has to go up."

However, I think it's important for beginners to get an idea of what the other methods of jumping are. Maybe one of those is best for you.

And remember, the approach to the bar is just as important as going over it. If you don't make a good approach, you won't get over.

But once you've accomplished that, don't stop. Many great jumps have been ruined when the bar has been knocked off by a careless movement of the arm or leg.

The Fosbury Flop

The Long Jump

THE LONG JUMP is one of the oldest track and field events. It combines both running and jumping skills.

I have personally always enjoyed the long jump. It was one of my favorite events.

In some ways the long jump is similar to a sprint. You need both speed and spring to be a good long jumper. The fast runner who can't get up in the air won't do well in the event. And a good jumper who doesn't have the speed to get a fast start won't succeed either.

Actually, you need all of the basic sprint movements in the long jump. You have to keep your knees high as you approach the takeoff board and your arms swinging at your sides.

Many coaches use check marks when teaching how to broad jump. This is good for some people, but I've never found it useful for me. I feel it's better to concentrate on jumping rather than looking for check marks.

The only check mark I ever used was a distance marker. The distance of the run up can vary greatly with jumpers. Some need a longer distance to reach top speed—more than 100 feet. Others need only 50 or 60 feet. The important thing is to reach your maximum speed a few steps before you get to the takeoff board.

I think the best way to determine the distance you will need is to stride through the event. Start about 60 feet away and run through it. See if you can reach full speed by the time you get to the board.

If that isn't far enough, try 70 feet. Keep moving back until you find your distance. Once you do, make a mark at that point so you'll know where to start.

Then go back to the principles of sprinting. Make sure you get a good start and concentrate on running in a straight line. Keep your body under control at all times.

When you come to the takeoff board, get as high in the air as you can. If you don't get up in the air,

When you come to the takeoff board, get as high in the air as you can. Keep control of the body while you're in the air.

Make sure you come down on your toes. Stretch out at the finish and land with your weight forward.

103

you'll come down quicker than you want. The higher up you get, the better chance you have of jumping further.

Keep control of the body while you're in the air. There are several different things to do with your legs at this point, and you must find what suits you best.

Some excellent jumpers like Ralph Boston seem to run while they're in the air. Others, like Bob Beamon, who set the world record at Mexico City in 1968, tuck their legs under them. I think the basic thing is to keep your body under control so that you land correctly.

Make sure you come down on your toes instead of your heels. Landing this way gives you several extra inches—the length of your foot's instep—which you'll lose by landing on your heels. In the broad jump these few inches can make the difference between winning and losing.

Another thing about landing on the toes is that if you do lose your balance, chances are you'll fall forward and not lose any distance. But if you lose your balance on your heels, you're likely to fall backward and lose distance.

I believe that every athlete has one great effort in him.

You never know when it will come. For Bob Beamon it was in the 1968 Olympics.

I was watching him jump because he had trouble with fouls in qualifying and almost didn't make the finals.

But when he took off on his first jump in the final round, I knew he was going to set a world record. It just seemed like he stayed in the air forever. He got the maximum spring that enabled him to get high in the air, about 6 feet. He tucked his feet up under him and just kept going. I didn't think he was ever going to come down. It was the perfect jump.

Beamon was also an excellent runner. He could do the 100-yard dash in about 9.6. And his tremendous spring helped him here also, which is why he holds the world record.

Beamon didn't use check marks. But if you do, get your coach or a teammate to help you measure where to put them. The marks should be placed at about one-third of the distance from where you start and again at two-thirds of the way to the takeoff board.

Using check marks helps you hit the takeoff board perfectly with your left foot if you are right-handed.

Run through your jump and "check" your check marks. Make sure you come down on your left foot at the first check mark and again at the next one. This should help you hit the takeoff board with your left foot.

When you get near the board, shorten your stride

just a little, maybe 6 inches at most. This allows you to coil your body for the upward spring of the jump.

Use your arms to help get you up in the air. When you take off, push them back behind the body and pull your legs up underneath you. Then, use the jump that is best for you.

Maybe you should tuck your legs up underneath you or maybe keep them moving in the air. One method worked for Ralph Boston, another for Bob Beamon. They both won gold medals in the Olympics, which proves there's more than one way to succeed.

Another very important tip in the long jump is making sure you hit the takeoff board as far forward as you can without fouling. The further forward you hit the board, the more inches you'll add to your jump.

Fouling can be a problem. It almost cost me my chance to win the long jump in the 1936 Olympics in Berlin.

I had set the world record in a track meet for Ohio State a year earlier. I jumped 26 feet, 8¼ inches, a mark that remained the world record for more than twenty-five years.

But in the Olympics I was having trouble with the takeoff board. On my first 2 jumps in the preliminary round, I fouled.

I was slightly tired because I was competing in the trials of the 220-yard dash, which were being held at the same time.

All I had to do to make the finals was to jump a little more than 23 feet, something I had done many, many times before. But I fouled on my first 2 tries and only had one chance left. I was angry at myself to think I had come all the way to Germany and might not make the finals in one of my best events.

Just before my last preliminary jump, a young German contestant in the same event came over and introduced himself. His name was Luz Long.

He said he had been watching me jump and then made a suggestion: "Why don't you put a mark behind the takeoff board and aim at taking off from there? Then you will be sure not to foul. You still should be able to jump far enough to make the finals."

I followed his advice. I made a mark about a foot behind the takeoff board and concentrated on jumping from there on my final try.

I qualified for the finals with a jump of more than 24 feet.

In the finals I set an Olympic record on my second jump. Each contestant had 6 jumps in the finals.

On his fifth jump, Long tied my record.

But I broke that record on my fifth jump and then

broke it again on my final jump, which was 26 feet, 5⅜ inches.

That distance held up as the Olympic record until Ralph Boston broke it with a jump of 26 feet, 7¾ inches at the 1960 Olympics in Rome.

Luz Long and I became very good friends for the remainder of the Olympics. This was unusual because of all the talk about Hitler and his dislike for the black members of the United States team.

I never saw Luz Long again after the Olympics. He was killed during World War II. But I will never forget how much he helped me.

Hop, Step, and Jump

THE TRIPLE JUMP, or hop, step, and jump, becomes very popular during Olympic years because it's an Olympic event.

It is similar to the long jump except that it calls for more coordination and strength and less sprinting ability. As in the long jump, you take off with one foot. The difference is that you complete the "hop" by landing on the same foot that you took off from rather than on both feet as you would in the long jump.

As soon as the foot hits the ground, take the longest stride possible to set yourself up for the jump. For instance, if you take off onto your right foot, land on the right foot, and only on the right

Triple Jump—As in the long jump, you take off with one foot. The difference here is that you complete the hop by landing on the same foot you took off from rather than on both feet. As soon as the foot hits the ground, take the longest stride possible (the step) to set yourself up for the jump.

110

111

foot. The left one is kept up in the air and stretched out as far as possible to get the maximum distance with the "step."

In the triple jump, it doesn't make any difference whether or not you take a great hop if the step and jump are not equally as good. That's why the left foot must be kept off the ground on the hop to get the best distance on the step.

When the left foot comes down on that step, you are ready to jump. The jump is the most important part of the triple jump because it should provide the longest distance.

The motion is the same as in the long jump, where you hit ground firmly and then get up in the air as quickly as possible. Get as high as possible on the jump and keep your feet tucked underneath.

Try to land with your weight forward so that if you fall, you'll fall forward and won't lose vital inches because your hand hits behind your feet.

You can work on the basic principles of the long jump while preparing for the triple jump.

How far should you go in each part of the triple jump? That depends on the individual. The hop and step should be about the same distance, with the hop possibly a bit longer.

You can set a goal of about 12 feet on the hop, another 12 feet on the step, and then as close to 20 feet as you can come on the jump.

You may find that your distance will be a little better on one part of the triple jump than another. The important thing is to get the maximum effort into all three parts of the triple jump.

A Final Word

GOD HAS GIVEN everyone the ability to do something. It might be as a musician or a painter, a businessman or a teacher. He gave me ability to compete in track and field.

Once you discover where your ability is, you must concentrate on developing it.

I believe in the development of young runners. It is a learning process just like anything else in life. You have to work for what you get. It takes determination, dedication, and discipline to accomplish anything worthwhile.

I first became aware of track and field when I was a youngster in Cleveland, Ohio. After playing baseball in the daytime, we would get together on the playground after dinner. Just before the playground closed, we would run races.

Sometimes you won and sometimes you lost. If you lost to another boy, you worked hard to beat him the next time.

My first actual competition came in junior high school. My coach was Charles Riley. He selected the members of the track team for the school.

Each day, during gym class, he would have us run in races and time us. Then, after class, he would call the names of the boys who were good enough to be on the track team.

It was one of the proudest moments of my life when he called my name.

Coach Riley taught me how to behave. His influence on me and many other boys kept us out of trouble. Without his guidance, we could very easily have become wards of the state.

I first became aware of the Olympic Games in 1932, when I read about them in the paper. At that time, a California runner named Charley Paddock was called the world's fastest human. He held records in the 100-, the 150-, and the 300-yard dashes, which helped earn him that title.

Charley Paddock came to our school to speak and told us what a thrill it was to be in the Olympic Games.

After he spoke to everyone, Coach Riley invited me into his office to meet Charley Paddock.

Afterward, Coach Riley asked me what I thought of Paddock. I told him I thought Paddock was a great man. And then I told him that I wanted to be known as the world's fastest human.

I asked Coach Riley what it would take to accomplish that. He told me about determination, dedication, and discipline. He told me it was a ladder you climb, not just in track but in everything you do in life. Whenever I felt I wasn't doing the right thing, I would go back to my coach for guidance.

If properly motivated, you can achieve the goals you seek. But it is important that a youngster listen to only one coach. He can tell you the fundamentals and then you build on that. If you follow these guidelines, there is a chance for greatness.

In 1932, when I was a junior in high school, after the Olympic Games in Los Angeles there was a series of track meets.

One of them was in Cleveland, and I was invited to take part. There were runners from Germany and Italy and other countries.

None of the great sprinters came to the meet and I was lucky enough to beat the ones who did compete in both the 100- and 200-meter races.

It was after winning in that meet that I thought I might have a chance to compete in the Olympics.

As a senior in high school I set four national records in an interscholastic meet in Chicago. The next year I enrolled at Ohio State.

I was very fortunate to do well there. In 1935, with the Olympics just a year away, I set 4 world records in a meet against the University of Michigan.

In college I learned the proper way to prepare for a meet. We were competing in track almost the year round. We would start in November with just light running and exercises to get in condition.

Then, in December we would train a little harder to be ready for the indoor season in January and February.

The important thing at that time was to make sure that taking part in track was fun. We didn't want to lose our desire by spending too much time practicing.

I believe that you can accomplish more in 45 minutes of practice if you work hard than you can in 2 hours if you don't train properly.

It's like anything in life. It has to be fun. I hate to see youngsters who lose interest in sports. It happens too often in Little League baseball, for example. The youngster is pushed so hard to win that by the time he gets to high school, he doesn't want to play baseball any more. That is bad. Competing in anything should be fun.

I think a word should be said about women competing in track and field.

It's a wonderful thing. Women don't lose their femininity when they compete in track and field; in fact, they develop poise, grace, and confidence from the experience.

Why deny someone a chance to compete in track and field because of sex? I really think that women have made more progress in track and field than men have over the years. The U.S. women's team did a tremendous job in the Olympic Games. Look how well Babe Didrikson did in Los Angeles in 1932, and Wilma Rudolph in Rome in 1960.

It takes concentration and dedication to excel in sports. There are always diversions—cars and television and dances and movies. But if you want to excel in track and field, or anything else, you have to be willing to make some sacrifices. That's where discipline comes in.

When you compete in track and field, you have to have a schedule. When I was competing, I had a weekly schedule and I stuck to it.

Monday would be an easy day I used for loosening up. I would run some 300s very easy. And then I would do my exercises to stay loose. I would finish up by running a few easy wind sprints.

Tuesday was a tougher day. I worked on my

starts, which would be used in both the dashes and the hurdles. I usually made about 15 starts.

Sometimes we had bullets for the starter's pistol. If we didn't, we had someone clap two-by-fours together to make a sound like a gun.

After I worked on starts, I would run some more wind sprints. After each sprint, I would jog back to the starting line. You didn't walk anywhere when you were on the field.

Then I would run three or four 220s at about three-quarter speed. Afterward I worked on the hurdles. I practiced the start and then went over the first 2 or 3 hurdles to make sure my steps were correct.

I would do this maybe 10 times. Then I would jog a little and that would be it. I wouldn't work on the broad jump at all on Tuesday.

Wednesday would be the same as Tuesday, except I added the broad jump, which I would run through a few times to make sure my steps were right.

Thursday was a light day, just to warm up and stay in condition. I would do lots of jogging and some sprints but not at full speed.

Then the trials for most meets were on Friday and the finals on Sunday. On the day of the meet I would do my exercises and then just stay loosened up.

That was my routine. I think that my success was

partly because I followed it faithfully. All of the work I put in for so many years finally paid off in the Olympics.

It was worth it. I remember standing there at the start of the 100-meter dash in Berlin. It was one of the most exciting moments of my life.

I looked down that track at the finish line 100 meters away, and I thought to myself that this was what I had spent so much time getting ready for.

I thought about the number of years I had worked, and the people who had helped me. I thought about the home I had come from.

Then I looked down at the uniform of the United States that I wore.

This was to be my moment of truth.

And after the race, which I was fortunate enough to win, I remember climbing up to the top of the victory stand.

I watched my flag, the American flag, rise above all others, and I heard my national anthem playing.

On that day, at that moment, I looked up to the heavens and thought, today I am an Olympic champion.

Determination, discipline, and dedication had paid off.